Frédéric Delalot

washingtonias and zoetropes 12

KDP Editions

First images, full of pages

We will talk about chances...

From continents...

On the grass

From the island...

Summer...

Wise lawns...

Sometimes, declining messages

Slightly, in an innocuous style.

In ecstasy...

Vis-à-vis the world

Sea bar...

Then the road...

It was the end of July...

A few days...

Everything had its solution

In the background of the décor

Without realizing it...

Maybe another time...

House in the distance, cove, and one night...

Raising dust from the winding tracks...

Still the youth...

Unspeakable years...

There was a time...

Night of all hours

This euphoria...

A pond, rocks, then our desires...

One time, we would look at the squares

Between the chapters...

Alleys lined with exoticism...

Smooth hair...

It was the unknown which guided...

Rapprochement of the nascent holidays

Unique, a few hours...

We realized our game

Nothing is done for everyone

Under a radiant sky...

First images, full of pages

Moments at once...

We look a bit like them...

Energy confidence...

Like a cycle...

First Human History

Gradual deviation...

Of the totality...

The integrity of several Stories.

Chronology...

From Human History...

Twenty-fourth century...

We may remember less

We will talk about chances...

Indefinite units...

Within this disbelief

New texture...

Gestural fluids

Through these doors...

Virtual spaces...

Customary...

Before, they slept more...

In the center of remote fortifications

Very far...

I think...

Garance stammering...

Then we were talking

Minutes...

Decision...

These details are revealing

From one universe to another...

Temptation of men...

Metamorphosis...

Buildings...

From continents...

In a dream...

Zigzagging descents.

Several years...

Still separate us

Different actions...

From the constellation

From the Big Dog...

On the grass...

Double...

With woods

Numerous...

Here you are...

With the hand...

Printed texts

From the courtyard...

Armed dances...

Many peoples

At will...

Conquering...

Gigantic...

From the island...

And sometimes even

As a result...

We are at the extreme

So in a low voice...

With an Atlantean woman...

I write these lines...

Now dynasties...

And that night...

Free...

She was jumping out of the mists

Subtle progressions

Summer...

Dream come from...

Wanderings...

Variety of seconds...

Continuity of passions

Indomitable...

Will...

Caravan...

Vehicles

Sleepy...

Almost...

Naked...

In fits and starts

Between two pages

And alleys...

Wise lawns...

Giving up wandering...

Voluntary flights...

Go from line to line online

Believing in a dream...

Sometimes, declining messages

Zebra fringes at noon...

Boudragues to the port...

Absolute suns, pride...

Heights...

These coincidences...

Brushing...

Giant pine, satisfied.

I was listening

Freelance

The city...

Student...

There were lampshades...

Giants, newspapers...

She was running into the apartment

Elsewhere, we gladly brushed shoulders

Slightly, in an innocuous style

Exoticism...

Some listened to music

Incredible fascination...

Clear advantage...

Panoramic...

And continued, on the heights

Stories...

And he had sometimes...

The intensity of the variety

In ecstasy...

Appointment...

Friends...

Social experience

Holiday...

Projects...

The same year.

Road lined

Trees...

Emotion...

Magnificent...

First...

We loved each other so much

Free days...

Strange...

Vis-à-vis the world

Beyond reality

Nature, enjoyment...

To be there...

In the years...

Very young...

Where we had dinner...

Some summer evenings

Originally...

Artists' Circus

From the stage...

Sea bar...

Entrenched...

At the very bottom...

From a staircase...

At that time

Very friendly...

Some vehicle parked

Close to friends...

She and I were passing.

Circular plan...
Hallucinatory...
It was going pretty well

Then the road...
Adventure lovers
The hacienda...

Passage...
From our friends
Campus...

Chestnut Street...
A fourteenth of July
And in France...
At ease...

Worldwide...
Browse France
It was the end of July
After...

Like characters...
Landscapes, happy moments...
Habits erected as principles
And again...

Charming onlookers...
A few days...
Tiny writers
Meeting...

Their lust...
The look...
In secret...
See paintings

For one night
Or two...
World...
Interested me

More...
In Compiègne...
In Reims...
We had walked around.

Roaring Twenties...

Everything had its solution

Honey and licorice...

Wealth...

Tempting...

Comings and Goings

Space...

I will tell them

Maybe...

And a few wakes...

In the background of the décor...

Automatic colors...

Video players

Infatuation...

Again

Collection...

Books...

Montreal, already...

Extrapolations, terraces

Interfered, lascivious...

Domes...

Fortuitous emblems...

Doric buildings...

Quadrangular obelisks

First memory...

Years, maybe

Take a taxi...

The night passes...

Airport

Much further...

On the Place Royale...

Symmetrical houses

Passing in front...

Without realizing it...

Omen, places...

In the mornings...

Let it rain, let it sell.

Parties at other windows

Meetings, paintings...

In the distance the nightlife...

Fast, time is running out...

Roller shutters, a little rusty

Until nightfall...

Maybe another time...

Heights along the streets, perhaps...

Red signs, planted on the edge of streets.

Joys of an era...

Frontier of distant time...

The feast contained the unspoken

Rejoicing, travel...

I gave myself time to undertake

Shadows and lights...

As separate subjects...

Shape...

I sometimes came back from a building...

House in the distance, cove, and one night

Carefree young...

Reach the beaches...

Museum of memories...

Touching tirades...

The exaltation...

Lifting dust from winding tracks

Hidden inscription...

Covered with sand...

Universe, sailing...

Subliminal hue palette

Regenerate...

Under the nascent flakes...

Evening of festive times...

Later, overtaking parks

A thousand peaks, by the terminals...

Horizons, pleasant walk

Postures...

Around the blades...

It's there, true nature

Still the youth...

Joyful comings and goings...

A gathering that sang...

Bistro upstairs, a street of time...

Found, endless text reading

Memory and perception...

Space, different eras

A moment, a few hours...

Those words...

Funny thoughts...

Like the independence of a progression

Unspeakable years...

Room with swimming pool...

Ground floor of a fence

Unique background, go there...

On the way, flights of boudragues

Trees of the Moors...

Curtains, round, summer...

Very high, she wrote...

Nudities, long conversations.

Those months had passed.

Negligently...

There was a time...

Very strong complicity...

We were going out...

Magnetization and passage

Fainted years...

Fluid character...

Between Mount Royal...

And the River...

The facades, the distant

This growing azure...

Quiet road...

And quasi-enjoyment

Visual...

Dream colors...

Let yourself be invaded by a gesture

Night of all hours...

Together...

Light, sometimes...

I loved feeling fullness

Spaces...

Tree field

Kilometers...

Going there...

We could merge

Impenetrable fields

At the Baths, at the Bus...

At Eugène Patin...

She would remember

This euphoria...

Multidimensional

Happiness...

Tanned...

Salt water on the skin

We were going out...

Retrospective...

Artists...

Well covered...

Like explorers

Freedom, again...

Bridges, in the distance...

Villages...

The menu that closed the year

Gradually different...

The illuminated windows...

Shops closed, in the city...

A pond, rocks, then our desires...

Which crossed paths, background conversation

Appointments, many years later

History was fluid between us...

At the top of an exotic city...

Giant statues...

Embraced at Station C...

Black linen shorts, and already...

One time, we would look at the squares

I remembered...

Her face, eyes closed

Earrings...

As before...

Always, to fall in love with us

Perfume from other eras...

Always irrational...

Over there...

We were trying to create an atmosphere

Pleasant, more than once...

Brushing...

Distinguishing solitudes

And the roofs...

Between the chapters...

And the waves...

From a spring

Those moments

Later...

At times, I remembered...

Intimate deraisons, I remembered

Alleys lined with exoticism...

Towards rue des Taillandiers...

Greeting the houseboats...

Catch a glimpse of the cheerful groups

The distance brought me closer...

Old novels...

The park was expanding...

Enjoying the heat...

Dresses with nonchalance

And she offered herself to the sun

We were alone...

Around one o'clock in the morning...

With the hour when we embrace

Approaching...

A few years ago

I would have climbed the steps...

Kilometers, dark skin...

Elegant body...

Smooth hair...

Floating in the wind

A taxi...

An apartment

After the wait...

Friends...

Number of artists

Had been invited

Branches of the islands...

Ecstasy...

Caresses...

From Cap Nègre

I didn't know...

Where did the waves come from...

It was the unknown which guided

Experience Approver

From the day before...

A temporary distance...

Looked like laurels...

I started from an illusion...

Asking suggestions

Pleasure of earthly excesses...

She showed me a bikini there...

Silver, a lamé bag, a bedroom...

Music behind walls, normal life

Fish...

Exotic...

Simple people...

Outside, young revellers

Taste of reunion...

In the vicinity...

I had disappeared at times...

Rapprochement of the nascent holidays.

Changing life

And the alcoves...

Towers...

The eighties...

With strangers, sometimes

The parked car...

Unique, a few hours...

Interactive glows...

Suspended in a large veil.

Museum of Fuchsia Art...

In a distant way...

We realized our game

At the edge of the world...

On the road...

Exhilarating youths...

Our hours had been crazy...

To exist, feeling in height

Endless discussions

Green courts, movement...

Bizarre novels...

That we wouldn't have read...

A lot had changed

Sensual desires...

From a weekend...

A little idleness...

We had made coffee...

We had plans...

Ideas...

Nothing is done for everyone

And like that...

Life was enjoyment

Have a nice day...

Whispering...

Exciting beaches...

Barely sleeping...

Sand jubilation...

Discreet entrenchment.

14

Fly away the heckled universe

Mind-blowing billiards...

And she had been emotional

Under a radiant sky...

Happiness of the lights

In the evening, somewhere...

In the city, caressing at night...

Transparent tunic...

Yellow second hand, on a carefree background.

For all sorts of reasons...

General movement, truncated schedules...

Sometimes hilarious faces, which reflected each other

In the mirrors...

Mythical memories of youth

Seemed frightening joys...

Prosperity, novelties of a moment...

Unknown liqueurs, in appearance...

Nothing really changes...

Everything was an illusion...

We could no longer see after the end

From the lagoon strip...

Walks by the sea

France in the portholes...

At high speed...

Distant stories...

Flew into the street...

Naked and thoughtful looks

The originality of desires...

Imaginable, the epochs

For a mystical reason...

By chance, autumn...

Hugs, later...

Packed our unique universe

A day here, a night there...

Dreamlike landscapes...

And an era she had not known

Past ideas...

15

Exit from a park, a playground

Classic sweatshirt...

Then the slope became discovered

Passages amazed...

Young partygoers, mini-shorts

In silver lamé, playful screams

Time had been gradually out of sync

Trillions of years...

Huge galaxies...

I drew happiness from the heart of memories

Incredible atmosphere...

Foreign eras...

We wanted to explore again...

In the evening or on the plains...

Innocuous, which the open sea calls

This energy...

Trajectory...

Virtual reality...

Robotic sex...

The time by the way...

Trust these screens.

Then quickly...

Soaked up what needed to be

Badges victories...

Otherwise nothing...

Absolute episode...

Programming of the blades

Sequences taken away...

Intrepid cadences...

And afternoons...

For other holidays...

Or other places...

Caresses of the moment

The towers...

Stood out...

In the evening...

The beauty of the landscapes...

16

I was listening to the blue orange beat...

Winged passages, lyrical paintings

Manias of passers-by...

Snippets of conversations

Quotes from readings

Of memories...

I remember those doors

Slammed, in a hurry, warm...

Exchanges, effects...

An evening of jubilation...

Spring...

We never got tired

To go around...

Contours...

Curious refinement

A lot of people...

Happiness of appearances...

Feeling of joy...

I went to the domes...

Metamorphoses of time

Gateway of yesteryear...

Springs started again...

In the night, her naked body...

The trees outside, I remember...

I was coming out of a building, a house

Almost at dawn...

Interludes no longer mattered

Like flying papers...

Other freedoms would advance...

I was wondering...

Near the cacti...

Love on the ground

Years passed...

Beyond the Universes

From time to time...

Vast cities...

Time on the lips...

17

The wind in the trees

Their dreams, their ideas

Most beautiful victories...

Ancient games

At the cutting edge...

Northern...

Winners...

Completed arpents

Pure joy.

The idea-force in extenso...

We were heading south...

As soon as you talk to the mirrors

Idle, sometimes I kept going...

From boudragues to the port...

I wanted to untie the fabrics...

A thousand years, far from the fallen leaves

Gold dust...

Close to green, climbing plants

Or in a hurry, intoxicating stories...

The long time...

In the summer darkness...

And beautiful...

And yellow...

Pinkish...

In places

Grows...

I always had a book...

By hand...

Muffled noise from cars

In the city...

Daily releases

Trends rubbed shoulders...

Indigo lighting...

By shifting the outlook...

Icy island, for a moment...

The unbelievable horizons...

Marinated, soaring music.

18

We were both looking at the park

The infinity of the global mind...

An inner, parallel world...

Birds that flew away

Between the trees...

It was a little early...

Then, on the simple side of the light

Under a slow sky, the background and the form...

Were reintegrating their future...

Encryption in stone, from hour to hour...

And I liked to go to bed late, delay my sleep

We were driving, we were getting lost on the way...

She threw herself out of the mists, from the worlds...

I started from an illusion

Full of breath...

Next to a text...

Or other nights...

Appearance of several...

Yesterday seems to me nearby...

Years go by

Vibrant passenger happiness...

Time-oriented...

We left at the end of the night

Fragrant, ruffled, still hot...

And there were green paths...

Between the houses of the neighborhoods...

Peaks of consumable periods...

I was traveling back in time, there were nights

How many parks, in how many spaces...

Galaxies to come...

New civilizations

Perfect harmonies...

That's the time...

Endless nights...

With our emotions

And our attractions...

Found...

19

In the distance, I saw Paris

We listened to France Info

Muted...

Flowers found in a book

Whose perfume intoxicates you...

New surroundings...

Thousands of kilometers...

Enjoyment...

We were talking about all things.

As in a strange dream...

A few hours passed...

It was yet another time

Chance and appointment...

America on the heights...

Flights and desires...

Life was vast...

And the weather seemed delicious

Arrangements...

With multiple atmospheres...

Relaxed with art...

Sometimes we stayed in the car.

Close to indoor courts...

Quiet spaces...

To get drunk...

We listened to electro-funk

We were going out...

Free spaces...

To be interpreted

Emotions...

From a youth...

Gentle parallels...

Paths...

Which overlooked

On the road

The trees...

The light...

The thought...

20

During the holiday season...

I saw a majestic fir tree

Images of wanderings...

I remembered the branches...

Which stretched up to the sky...

Graffiti on brick walls

Nonchalant beaches...

Pictures of crocodiles

And barracudas...

Over there...

In the early morning...

On the Square...

Two white containers remained

A Sunday afternoon

From February...

In the middle of the years...

Nineties...

The chalet...

And other facilities

Would be dismantled...

Quickly...

She would have reprogrammed itself

For the evening...

Music in space...

Light...

Everyone was trying...

To exist...

Dense crowd...

And almost family

Now and then...

Or in places...

Wandering beach

Royal flags

Spheres of different colors...

Above the happy days...

A festive air, Japanese surfer

Journey in words...

21

Memories arose

In the winter...

See parties...

At the other windows...

See paintings...

Taking the same paths

And I walked along the shops

Hadn't we already wandered...

In other times...

Colors out of the blue...

Kind of purple dream...

Of fuzzy and pleasant dream...

Which put the comings and goings to sleep

To continue...

The moment...

There were ink and beauties

In a hurry...

Trees *enguirlandés*...

Sparkling fir trees...

As with multiple filters...

That we applied to the same photo.

We walked along the bar...

Located in a first room...

Fainted rays...

Before going to the beaches

Under the Sun of Dreams

And enthusiasms...

Scattered loves...

There were games...

History memory...

Linen sheets...

In the meanders...

A night of escapade

Brisk walking...

Next day...

Snowball of the Castle

And small maple leaves.

22

I was going up the stairs

Cinder blocks...

The plaster paths...

Turn...

Impalpable...

From a megacity

Maps

At the morning wheel...

From a car...

Maybe tracks, inspiration...

Psychic cut-outs...

From an appropriation...

Escape routes of memories

The fresh foam splashed us

In the eyes of others...

We had no existence...

Out of the ordinary...

Sleeping passions...

Crystal bits of snowflakes...

Winter was cold...

Minutes in a hoodie.

Describe the places...

Remembering hypnotic motors

Connivances like that...

Balance between sweetness and bitterness

Minimal adornments, forget the logic...

And what had become of the stories...

We wanted to know a reassuring path

The wind swept the square and the snow flew...

Covered the streets...

And the sidewalks...

Stealth red lights

Purple glow...

Perfect setting for rapprochements

And cosmic calm...

All accessible...

Things were modelable...

23

He was turning on a blue light

Placed on a tablet...

Like a curious little...

Since the end of the century

At least I guess

Clean universe...

Built on sequences...

All the drunkenness, and its sinuous breaks

Bent down, happiness of our empires.

The escaped ways of memories...

White roads and fields...

The places where we were...

Perfumes of stories, whispered words

Remotely controlled...

Maybe...

Time is vast

At present...

Connivance of the rides...

I wanted to stay...

In retreat, to simply look

People and things...

The city...

Summer...

Relaxation

Recurring

And we were no different

Than others...

There were other generators...

Free ways of happiness...

Interiorities...

Automatic eroticisms, revivals...

In Bastille or elsewhere, and still a few nights

Deep down, I liked straight lines...

Unbeatable happiness...

There were worlds...

Happy transposition...

And later, a meditative era.

24

Small red lanterns

I saw worlds...

Sculptures...

Or virgin apartments

Between the blinds...

There was a canvas...

Psychedelic

At the front...

Colorful...

As in a strange dream

I longed for the big party...

Dense slow motion...

Formidable instops

We remembered the happy days...

And the festive moments...

Innocuous details reminded me of other details

Everything was white and quiet, fantastic...

Came from other times...

Desire to be in the rhythm of the night...

Top of the towers...

The Ferris wheel turned pink, then blue.

The Ferris wheel was mandarin

There were garlands...

In the trees...

We couldn't do everything again...

That was a long time ago

Unexpectedly...

Hours of lights...

And joy...

Scattered...

We were listening to Talk Talk

One night...

So many memories...

Vanilla creams...

Chocolate...

Popular songs

On the fourteenth of July...

25

Some nights she had a tunic

I left things to themselves...

And elsewhere everything was different...

I settled into the narrative

With a kind of slowness...

In space and time...

And I loved the sunsets...

And this purple, purple halo...

As if the years had not passed.

I had remembered a long vacation

Roads, continuous comings and goings...

It was simple...

And at the end of a steep bend...

Desire for endless excitement...

We were in fluid fabrics

Hot rays...

In memory dimensions

Where we had managed to imagine a sequel

Splendid, sometimes youthful...

Eternal youth of the years...

Innocuous victories...

Canvases of the dawn...

Energetic, immortal...

Free, earthly figures...

And you took me to the bubbles of Java

Young busts of the roulades...

Hundred years...

A long time ago, at the time

Ingenious holidays...

Intoxicating doors

Blue light...

The immense dawn

Trophies...

Only way to enjoy...

My dreams were rushing

Aftermath...

Summer as elsewhere...

26

Potential for a renaissance...

The night, when words get drunk

Travel interiors, soothing

We were still thinking about these volutes...

Aliens, in the halo of blinds

Tiny memories of the sea...

Freedom, inexhaustible energy...

Anthem of the sails, the Roaring Twenties...

Passing happiness, countless possibilities.

The honey ponds were just a moment...

Azure walls, I remember a young road...

They just wanted a few good times

And all the clothes of yesterday, mirages...

Roads...

We were together...

Undressed...

By the beauty of a cove

From a heaven, hope...

Like deep memories

Unreal happiness...

Laps, we were heading south...

And we were back...

In a village of stones...

I don't know if the clock was ticking

Palm trees to the ships...

The coasts...

As I saw your lips...

Laziness and privilege

Burst out of full pages...

Life was simple, collected our thoughts

Heads down to ensure a bust...

Young wandering, memory of countries...

The races were just a kind of summit

You have to believe in the light, really...

I wondered where the assumptions were going...

Distant ecstatic, yesterday, parade of moments, this almost nothing

On the heights of an Anse, we loved roulades...

27

O many dials...

I remember...

Logic illuminates the cliffs

Long...

The sap of ancient times...

In a high cabin

Eight thousand years separate us

Remote fortifications...

Very far from the hyperpoles...

The old places appeared...

Ostentatious pomp of our feelings

In the crowd, with a delight

From the new century...

How many nights, how many days

In one dimension, something

Refined, far away, there...

In a world...

Come to think of it, fantasy...

Baroque, Bohemian troupes

Encrypted voices...

Slowly, singular idea...

In the light of the mutants, yesterday...

Bouquets of flowers, evasions

Caress of triumphs...

A few pages...

I was reviewing my nights

Like a youth

Rainbow could be heard

Casual branches

Rapprochements...

Esplanade, tapas...

In other worlds...

Exhilarating times

June fever...

Tall towers...

Distracted...

With tranquil landscapes.

We stopped the car

In famous speed...

Swagger...

Wooded islands...

I put on a t-shirt

Wider tracks...

Relieved of ambitions...

From the crowd...

He really existed.

An illusion escapes...

In dreamlike music...

To I don't know what whole world

Towards somewhere else...

Feeling of adventure

Hotel room...

Transparent vials

From a summer sky...

Millennia...

A thousand pages ahead of us...

Through intermittency

From the heart...

Eroticisms...

Automatic...

Revivals...

And still a few nights

Without too many people...

Unbeatable happiness

And the joys...

There were worlds

And later...

Through the vegetable gardens...

Small red lanterns

I saw worlds...

Between the blinds...

At the front...

In a story...

I longed for the big party.

Dense slow motion...

Elusive moments

In memory...

It was snowing...

It was snowing...

Everything was white

There were slight smiles

Desire to be in the rhythm

From the night...

The Ferris wheel turned red

Young...

Tangerine...

There were garlands...

In the trees...

That was a long time ago...

Processions of new data

Diffuse lighting...

Hours of lights

Scattered...

To the domes...

So many memories...

Some nights...

Some nights...

I left things

To themselves...

Everything was going to become...

I settled into the narrative

In space...

And time...

And I loved sunsets

Facing the sea...

Long holidays...

The continual comings and goings...

At the end of a bend...

Steep...

And desire interfered...

Endless excitement.

Light of centuries, sometimes...

Metropolises, respite found...

The trip offered us the alcove

Fickle flowerbeds

Freedom was there

Between pages...

On the side of the nomads...

With the stones of yesteryear...

I marked the date at the top.

We superimposed the clothes

Inner courtyard, transparent...

Road, landscapes...

First love...

As long as we believe in it...

By imagining other landscapes...

We loved the heart of time

In the city...

Obsession...

To the oaths...

First Impressions

Of joy...

Hours...

Passed...

Train...

Open House

To illusions...

Magic of change

At the beginning of year...

In the evening...

Past evenings...

To remake the world

To the hotel...

Mirrors in the night

We crossed paths in the night

Evasions, arid happiness

With an accommodating hue...

Escapades...

Music...

Lights...

Seaside

Landscapes of grace...

Dizzying pretext

From this floating...

Timeless dimension

Which encompassed...

Broken with centuries...

Sometimes other freedoms would advance

Emerging from tesserae...

Sandy mist...

Slow motion of private foliage...

The variations...

Top of the images...

On repetitive notes

Art reassured...

We are now on an island

The process is up to me...

Essential...

I went through the weeks...

I sometimes came back

At a glance...

Bohemian...

Mixture...

I had gone...

In the sense

General...

Of the future...

Lights...

Luxurious...

Notebooks...

Reflection of the years

A very long time ago...

One evening...

Deep...

Where the landscapes change.

I remember...

Ostentatious pomp of our feelings

I saw my nights again...

Wider tracks...

A thousand pages ahead of us...

Unbeatable happiness...

Desire to be in the rhythm

That was a long time ago...

And the desire interfered

On the side of the nomads...

Road, landscapes...

Mirrors in the night...

On the heights of an Anse, we loved roulades

Landscapes of grace...

Sometimes other freedoms would advance...

Luxury lights...